101 NUTTY NATURE JOKES

by Melvin Berger

illustrated by B.K. Taylor

SCHOLASTIC INC.
New York Toronto London Auckland Sydney

ISBN 0-590-47763-3

12 11 10 9 8 7 6 5 4   4 5 6 7 8 9/9

Printed in the U.S.A.   01

First Scholastic printing, April 1994

Ike: That's a friendly tiger. He'll eat off your hand.
Mike: That's what I'm afraid of!

What did the monkey say when his sister had a baby?

"I'll be a monkey's uncle!"

A man was driving through the jungle. His car broke down. An ape came over. "It's a dead battery," the ape said.

The man was very scared. He ran all the way back to camp. "An ape told me my battery was dead!" he panted.

"Don't listen to him," said his friend. "Apes don't know anything about cars!"

Bill: I met a gorilla who can play chess.
Jill: He must be very smart.
Bill: Oh, no. I beat him every time!

Is it hard to spot a leopard?

No. They're born that way!

Why shouldn't you ever tell a secret to a monkey?

Because they carry tails!

Why did the fish cross the ocean?

To get to the other tide!

Did you ever see fish cry?

No. But I once saw whales blubber!

Did you ever see a man-eating shark?

No. But I once saw a girl eating lobster!

How do you catch an electric eel?

With a lightning rod!

Why did the sailor throw a penny into the whale's mouth?

He thought it was a wishing whale!

Why did the whale eat two ships loaded with potatoes?

Because no one can eat just one potato ship!

First fisherman: Is this river good for trout?

Second fisherman: It must be. I've not been able to catch one!

What did the ocean say to the river?

"Nothing. It just waved!"

SILLY SNAKES

Why do you measure snakes in inches?

Because they have no feet!

What did the snake say after he bit the man?

"Fangs a lot!"

Did you hear about the two boa constrictors that fell in love?

They had a crush on each other!

What did the boy snake say to the girl snake?

"Give me a little hiss!"

Al: I found a baby snake.
Sal: How do you know it's a baby?
Al: I could hear its rattle!

An old proverb says, "A bird in the hand — makes it hard to blow your nose!"

What kind of cookies do birds like?

Chocolate chirp!

Why do hummingbirds hum?

Because they don't know the words!

Teacher: Isn't it wonderful how chicks get out of their eggs?

Pupil: It's even more wonderful how they got inside!

Ted: What kind of bird is that?
Fred: It's a gulp.
Ted: I never heard of a gulp.
Fred: It's like a swallow — but bigger!

Why do storks stand with one leg raised?

If they raised both legs they'd fall over!

Abe: That was a terrible storm last night.
Gabe: Why didn't you wake me up? You know I can't sleep during a storm.

It's so cold at the North Pole that —

- our candle froze and we couldn't blow it out!

- our words got frozen and we had to wait until summer to hear what we'd said!

Pam: London has more fog than any other city.

Sam: I was once in a city with more fog.

Pam: What city was it?

Sam: I don't know. It was too foggy to see the name!

Why did Benjamin Franklin enjoy
flying his kite?

It gave him a charge!

It was raining cats and dogs, and there
were poodles in the street!

What color is the sun?

Rose!

What color is the wind?

Blew!

What did the hurricane say to the tornado?

"Let's blow this town!"

Why did the camper stay up all night?

She was wondering what happened to the sun. Then it dawned on her!

Cindy: Why do elephants paint their
toenails red?

Mindy: I don't know.

Cindy: So they can hide in a
strawberry patch.

Mindy: I don't believe you.

Cindy: Did you ever see an elephant in
a strawberry patch?

Mindy: No.

Cindy: See. It really works!

Pa: I can lift an elephant with one hand.

Ma: I don't believe you.

Pa: Find me an elephant with one hand and I'll show you!

Why does the logger use an elephant to haul wood out of the jungle?

He saves money this way. The elephant works for peanuts!

What goes, "thump, thump, thump, squish . . . thump, thump, thump, squish"?

An elephant walking through the jungle with one wet sneaker!

Why do elephants have trunks?

Because they don't have backpacks!

Teacher: How do you keep an elephant from going through the eye of a needle?
Student: Tie a knot in its tail!

What do you call a flying elephant?

A Dumbo jet!

How did the elephant get to the top of
the oak tree?

It just sat on an acorn and waited!

What's the difference between an elephant and green peas?

Elephants don't fall off your fork!

Why is a chicken stronger than an elephant?

An elephant can get chicken pox. But a chicken can't get elephant pox!

What's big and gray and turns blue?

An elephant holding its breath!

Irv: Would you eat an elephant egg?
Merv: No. I don't like elephant yolks!

There was an old man with a beard,
Who jumped on a wild horse that reared.
His friend said, "Never mind,
You will fall off behind,
You silly old man with a beard!"

There once was a young man from Leek,
Whose nose became a long beak.
It grew quite absurd,
Till he looked like a bird,
And flew to the south in a week.

There was a young lady from Niger,
Who smiled as she rode on a tiger.
They came back from the ride,
With the lady inside,
And the smile on the face of the tiger.

POKY PLANTS

Which flowers are fun to kiss?

Tulips!

Which tree grows at the seashore?

The beech tree!

Which tree claps?

The palm!

Which tree doesn't play checkers?

The chess-nut!

Why did the farmer bury his money?

He said it would make the soil rich!

Which tree likes to eat ice cream?

The pine. It has lots of cones!

How do you know the willow tree is sad?

It's weeping!

Jake: This is a dogwood tree.
Max: How do you know?
Jake: By its bark!

Mother Lion: Junior, what are you doing?

Lion Cub: I'm chasing the hunter around the tree.

Mother Lion: Didn't I tell you not to play with your food?

How do you get fur from a lion?

Run fur away!

When does a lion relax?

When it's lion down.

Fred: What are you doing?

Jed: I'm hunting for lions.

Fred: But there are no lions around here.

Jed: That's why I'm hunting for them!

A man brought a lion back from Africa. One day he was walking with the lion on a leash.

A policeman stopped him. "You can't walk around with a lion. Take him to the zoo."

"Okay," said the man.

The next day the policeman saw the man and the lion again. "I thought I told you to take the lion to the zoo," he said.

"I did," replied the man. "Today I'm taking him to the movies!"

What's the difference between a lion who steps on a nail and a hurricane?

One roars with pain. The other pours with rain!

CRAZY CROSSES

What do you get if you cross a parrot
and a bumblebee?

*An animal that talks about how busy it
is!*

What do you get if you cross an ape and a skunk?

I don't know. But it would always get a seat on the bus!

What do you get if you cross a
porcupine and a sheep?

An animal that knits socks!

What do you get if you cross an octopus
and a cow?

An animal that milks itself!

What do you get if you cross a chicken and a duck?

A cheep quacker!

What do you get if you cross a pig and a pine tree?

A pork-u-pine!

What do you get if you cross a turkey
and a centipede?

A turkey with one hundred drumsticks!

What do you get if you cross a moth and a glowworm?

A moth that can see in dark closets!

FUNNY FROGS

What happens when a frog gets stuck in the mud?

It gets unhoppy*!*

What do frogs wear on their feet?

Open-toad *shoes!*

The frog is the only animal that doesn't mind if you say, "Go jump in a lake!"

To telephone a frog you call the *hop*erator!

A tall pile of frogs is a *toad*em pole!

Ted: My kid sister swallowed a frog.
Ed: Did it make her sick?
Ted: It sure did. She croaked!

What did one owl say to the other owl?

"I don't give a hoot!"

What did one robin say to the other robin?

"Ain't that tweet?"

What did one cow say to the other cow?

"I'm in the moo for love!"

What did one skunk say to the other skunk?

"So do you!"

What did one worm say to the other worm?

"Where on earth have you been?"

What did one frog say to the other frog?

"Hoppy *birthday!*"

NATURE NONSENSE

What did the beaver say to the tree?

"It's been nice gnawing you!"

The Amazon River has a big mouth!

Teacher: These rocks were brought here by the glacier.
Student: Where's the glacier now?
Teacher: It went back for more rocks!

Why do birds fly south for the winter?

It's too far to walk!

Tammy: I lost my pet parrot.

Sammy: Why don't you put an ad in the paper?

Tammy: Don't be silly. My parrot can't read!

How can you tell which end of the worm is the head?

Tickle it and see which end laughs!

What's the difference between a fly and a bird?

A fly can fly. But a bird can't bird!

Is it true that an alligator won't attack you if you're carrying a flashlight?

It depends on how fast you're carrying the flashlight!

A woman comes into a pet shop. She tells the clerk, "I want to buy a sweater for my pet chimpanzee."

The clerk says, "If you bring in your chimpanzee we can find the right size."

"Oh, no," says the woman. "I want this to be a surprise!"

Why did the fly fly?

The spider spied her!

What says, "Zzub, zzub"?

A bee flying backward!

Woman in Shoe Store: I'd like a pair of alligator shoes.
Clerk: Sure. What size is your alligator?

Gert: Where are the bugs during winter?

Bert: Search me.

Gert: No thanks. I just thought you might know!

Why don't pigs get sunburned?

They wear sun oink-ment!

Simon: Do you know it takes three sheep to make a sweater?

Pieman: I didn't even know sheep could knit!

What is on the ground and one hundred feet in the air at the same time?

A centipede lying on its back!

What does the banana do when it sees a gorilla?

It splits!

What did the proud firefly mommy say while watching her little son?

"Isn't he bright?"